Copyright © 2016 Swear Word Coloring Book

All Rights Reserved Worldwide

Swear Word Adult Coloring Book

Extremely Rude Sweary Stress-Relieving Coloring Book For Adults (Curse Words For Relaxation Featuring Animals & Random Inanimate Objects)

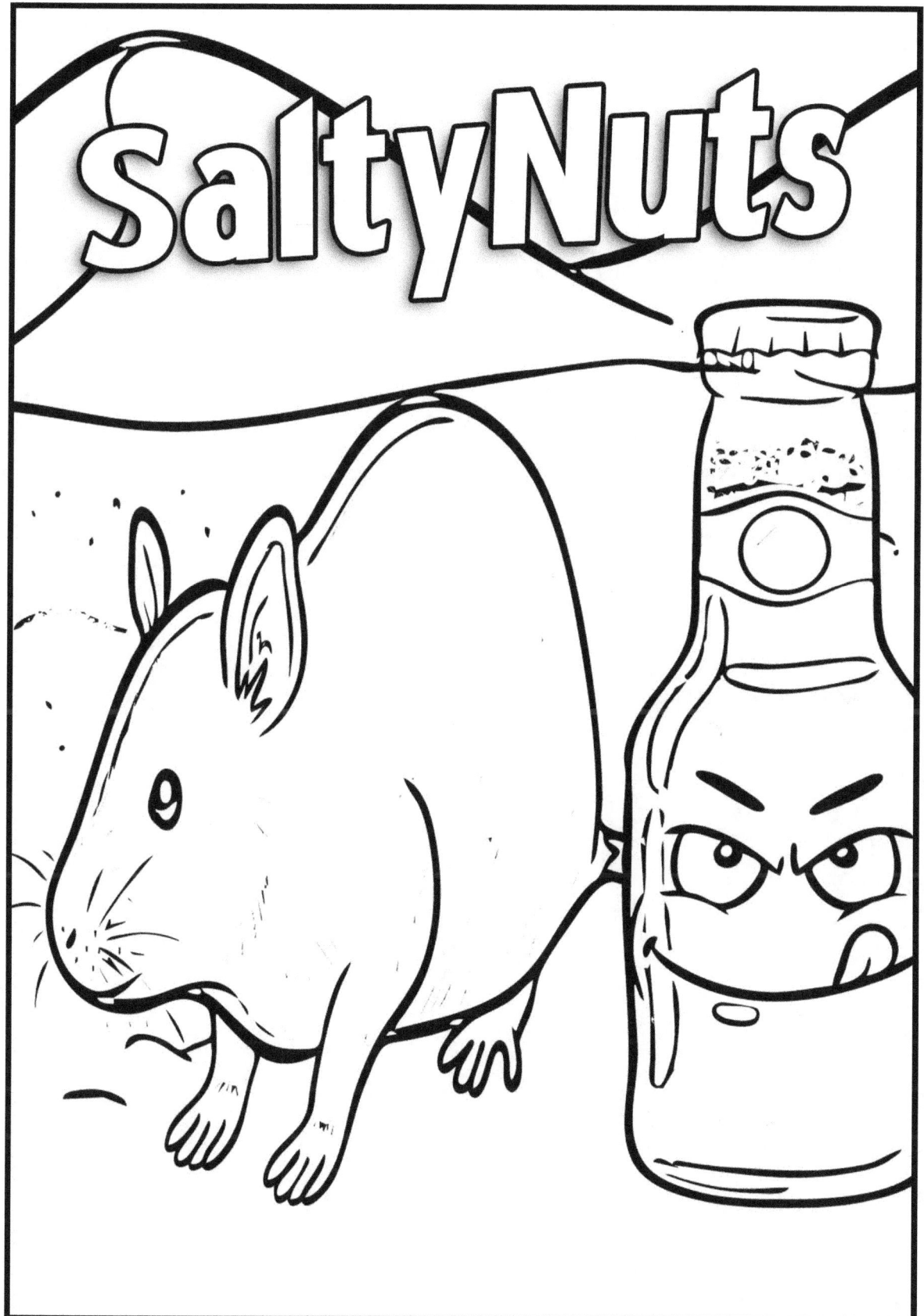

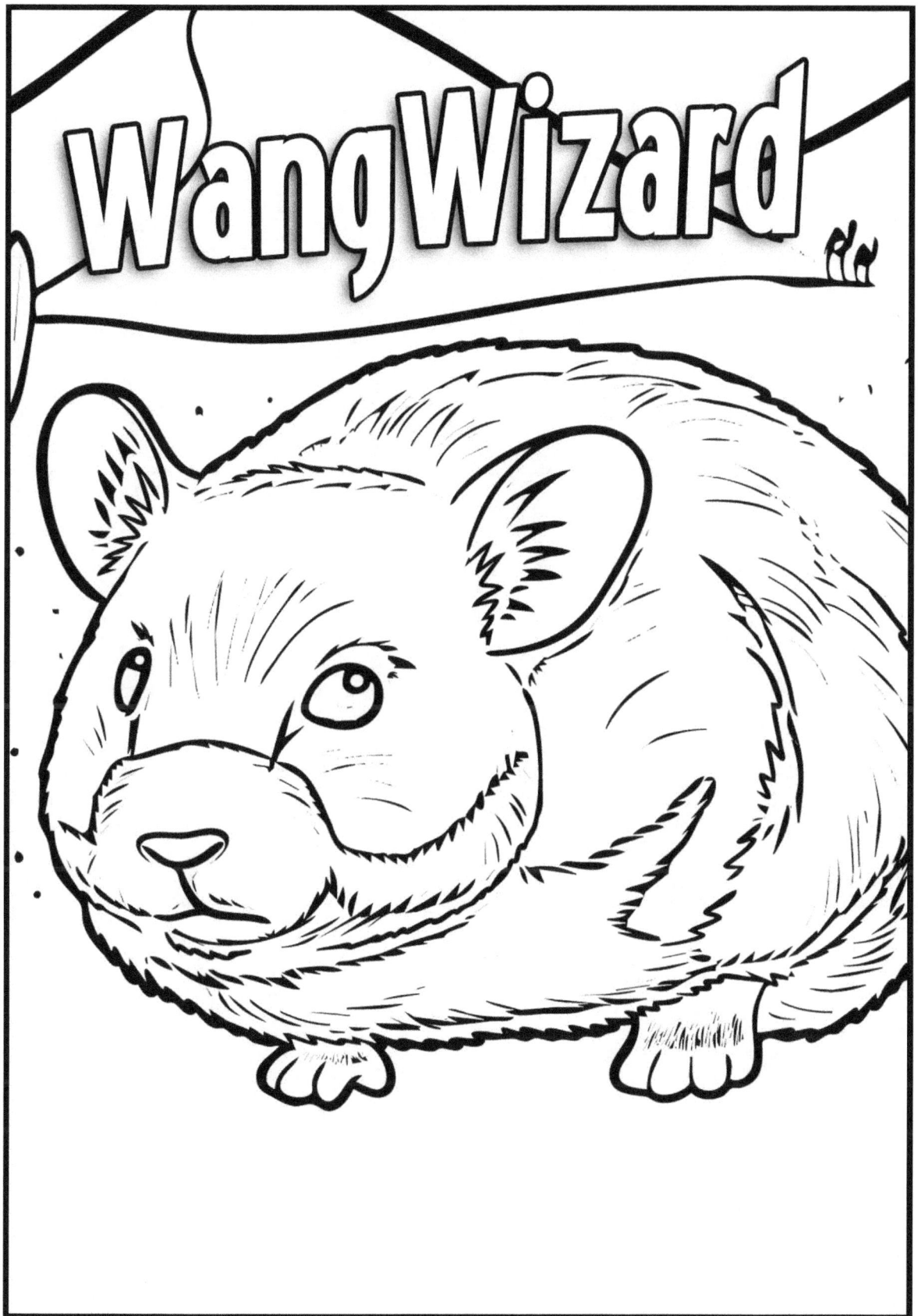

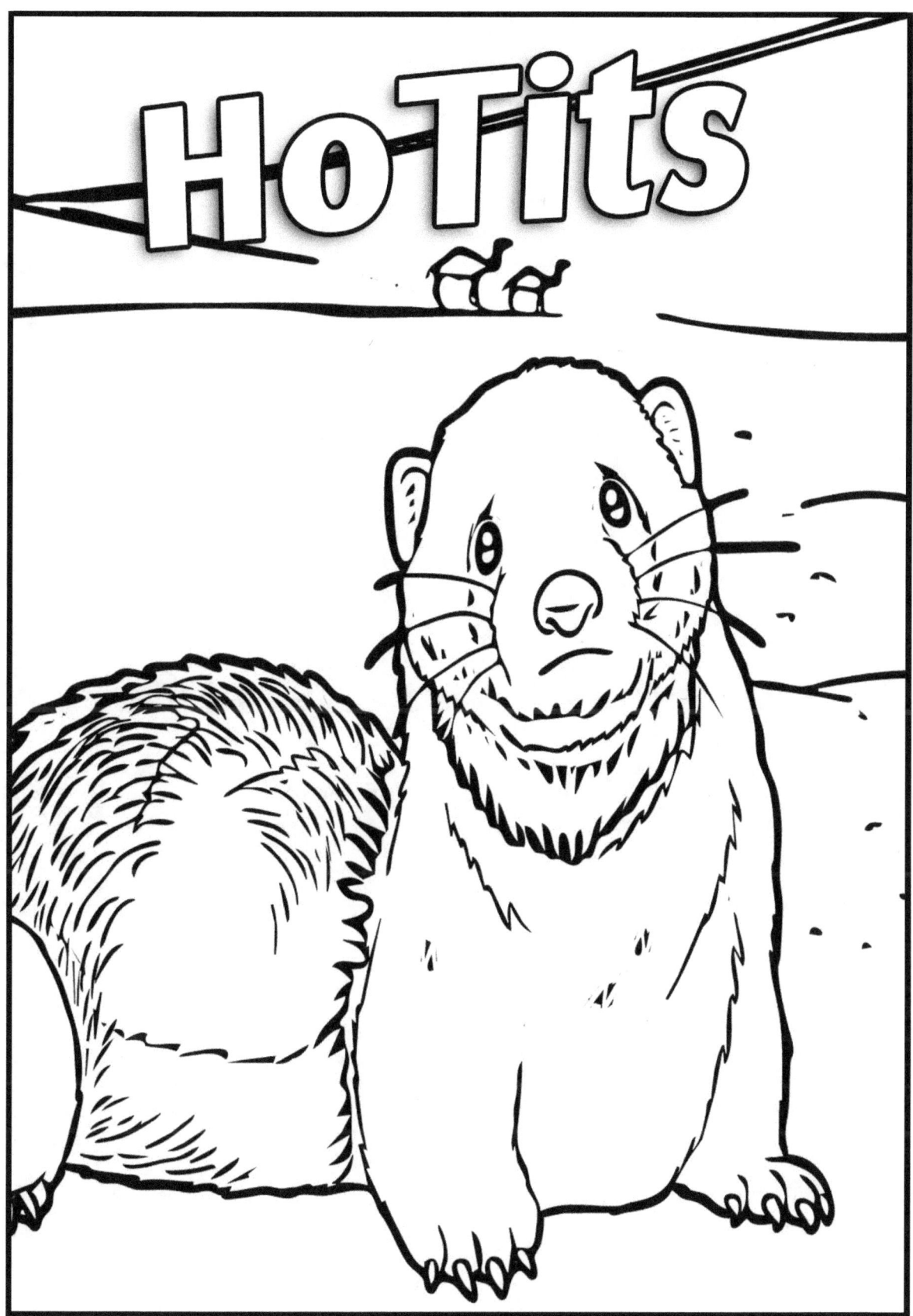

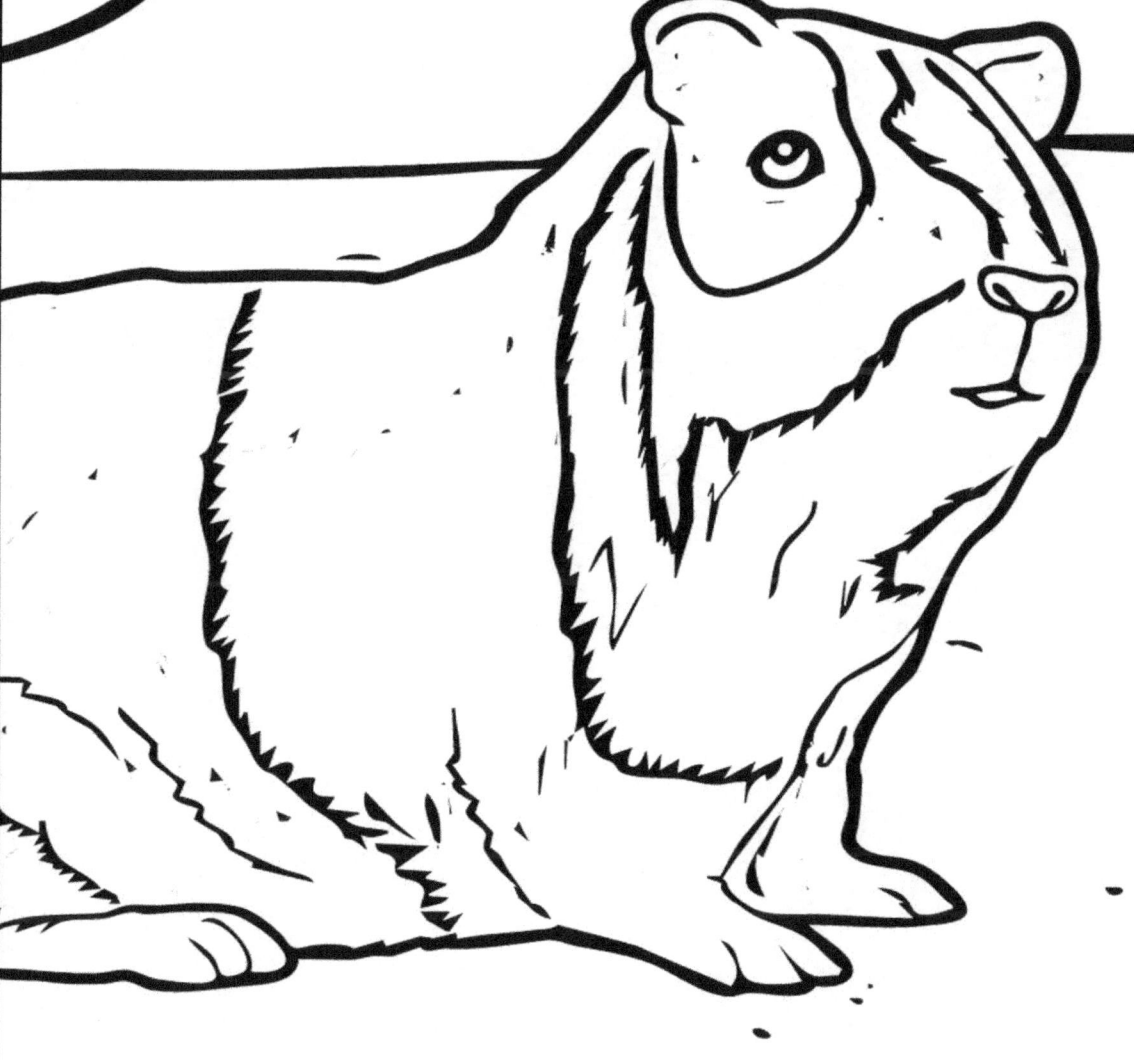

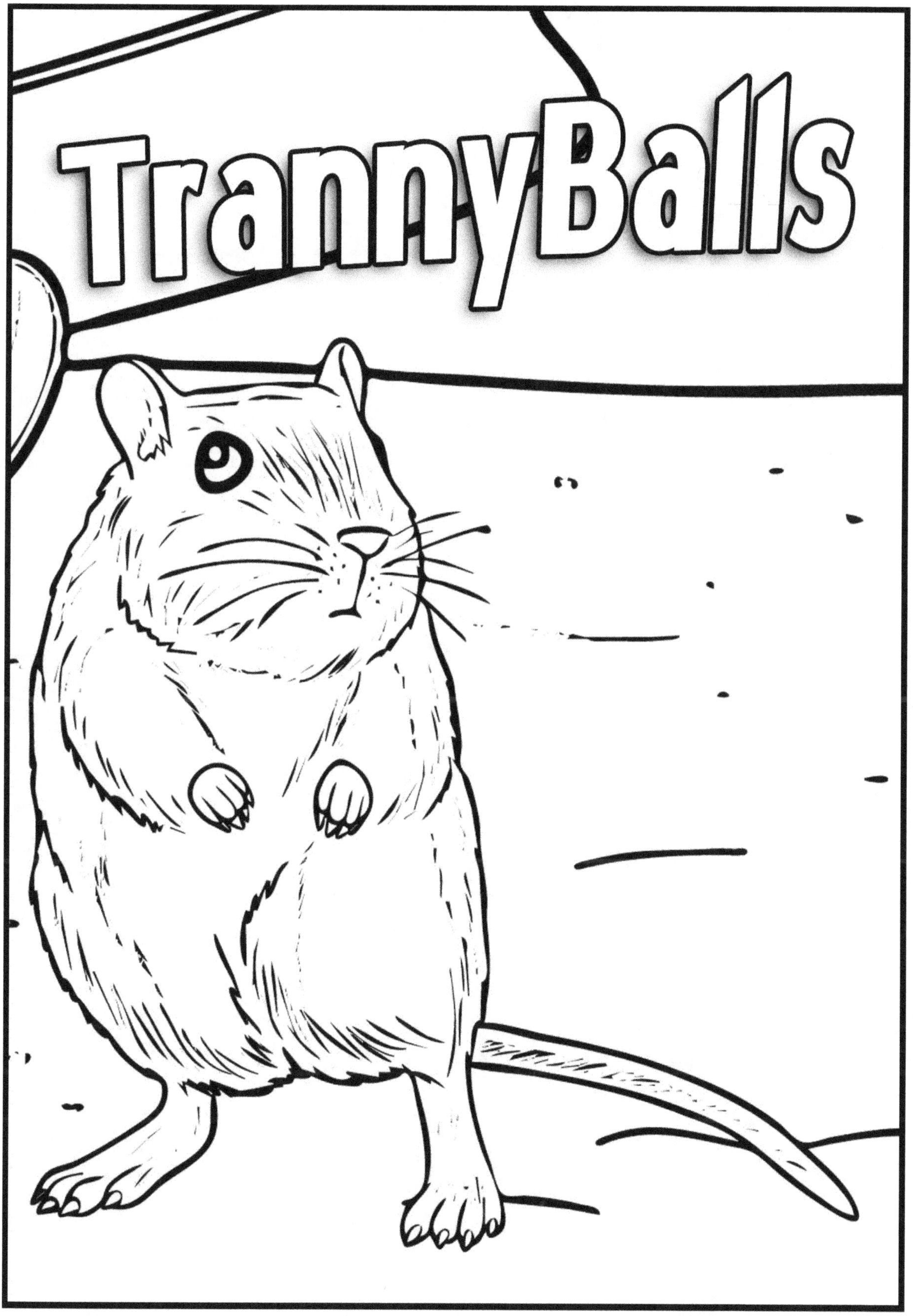
TrannyBalls

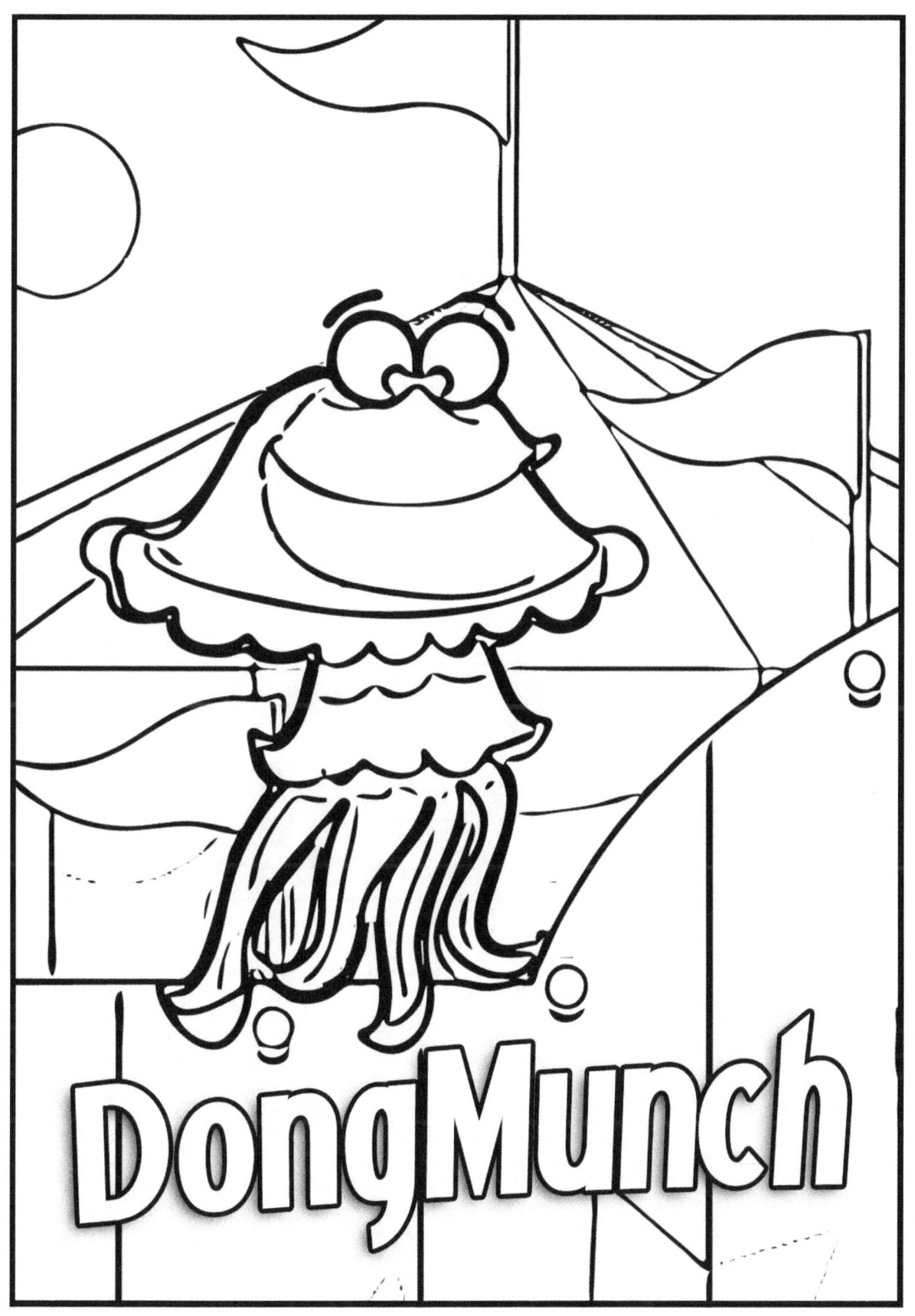

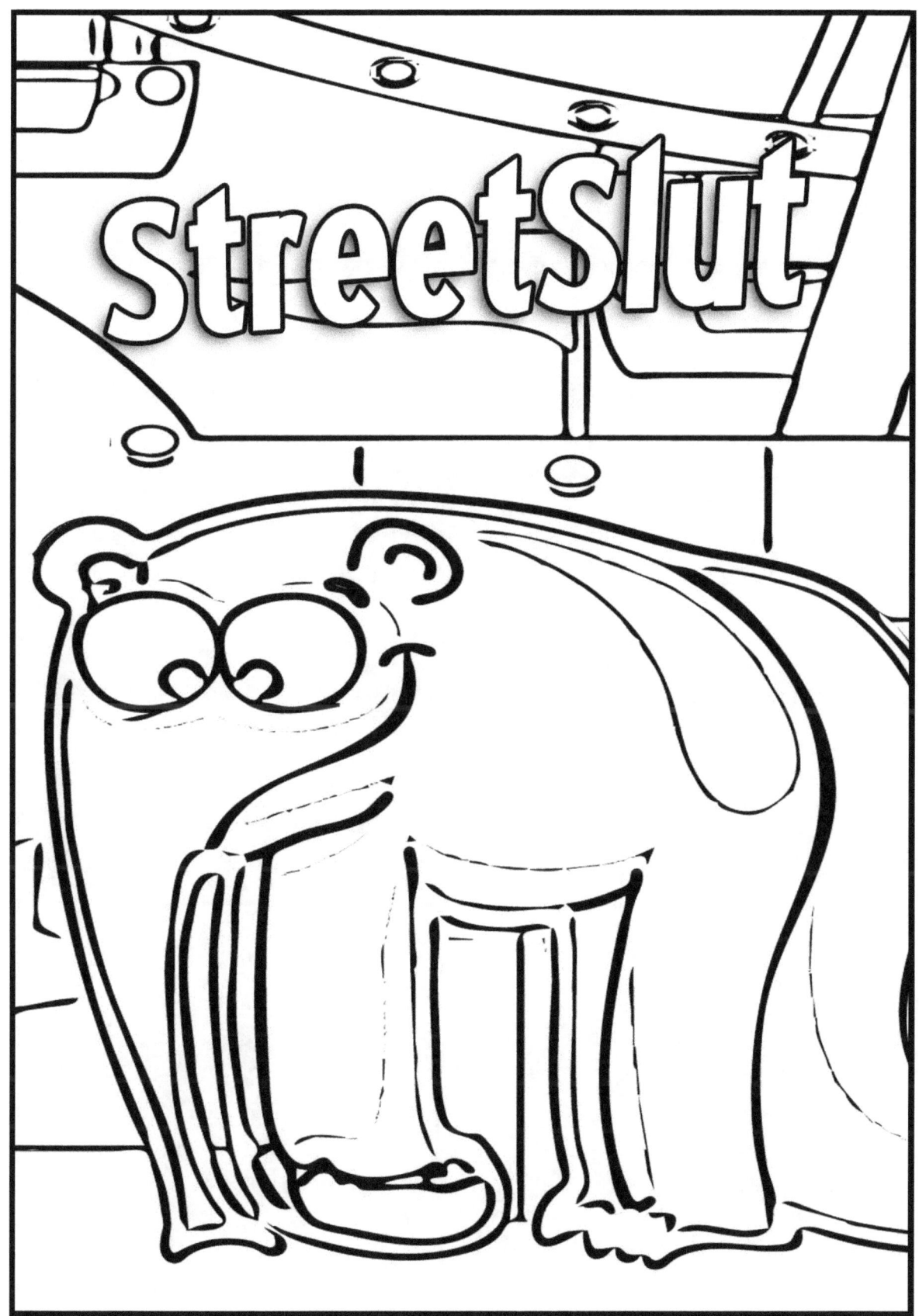

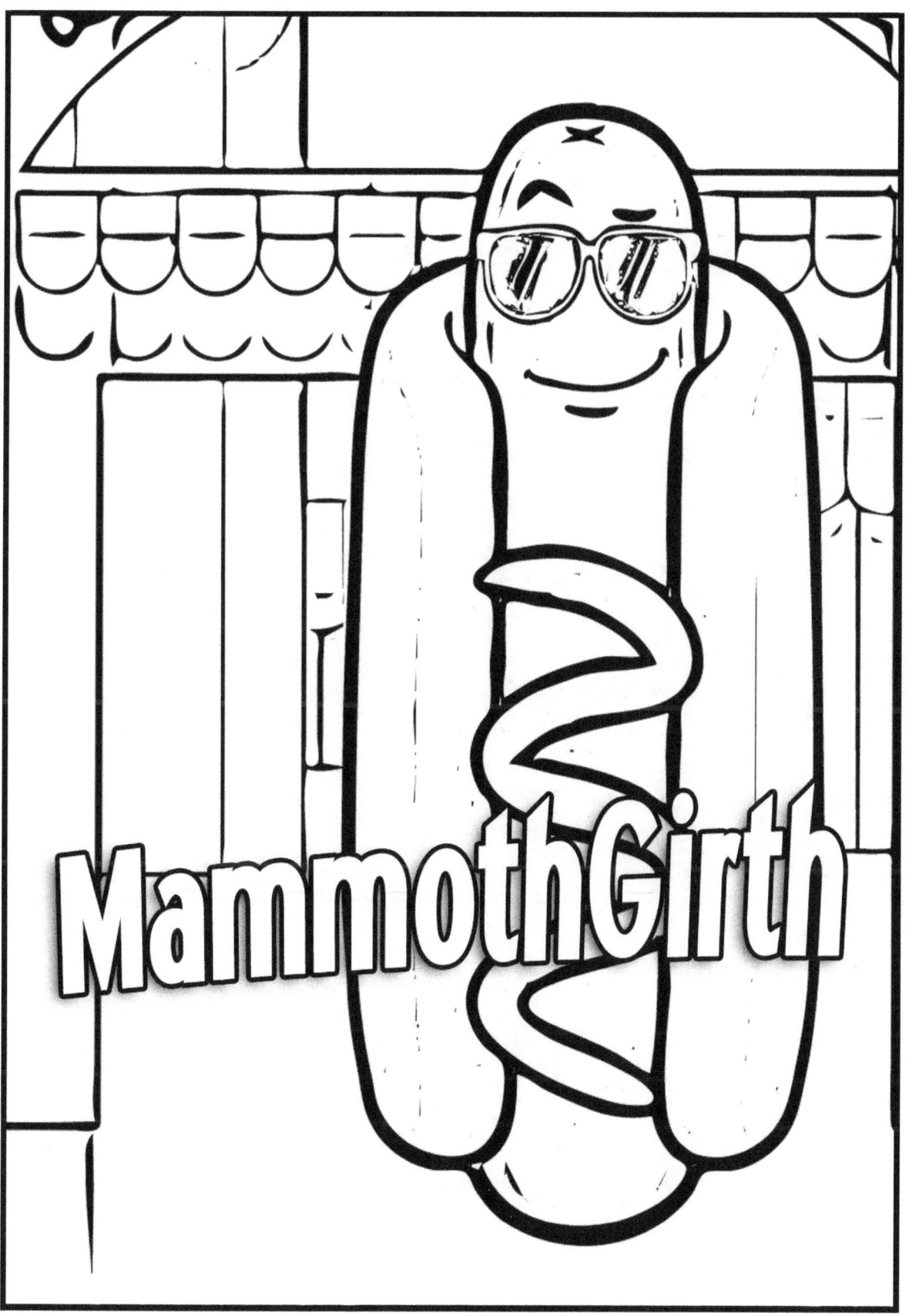

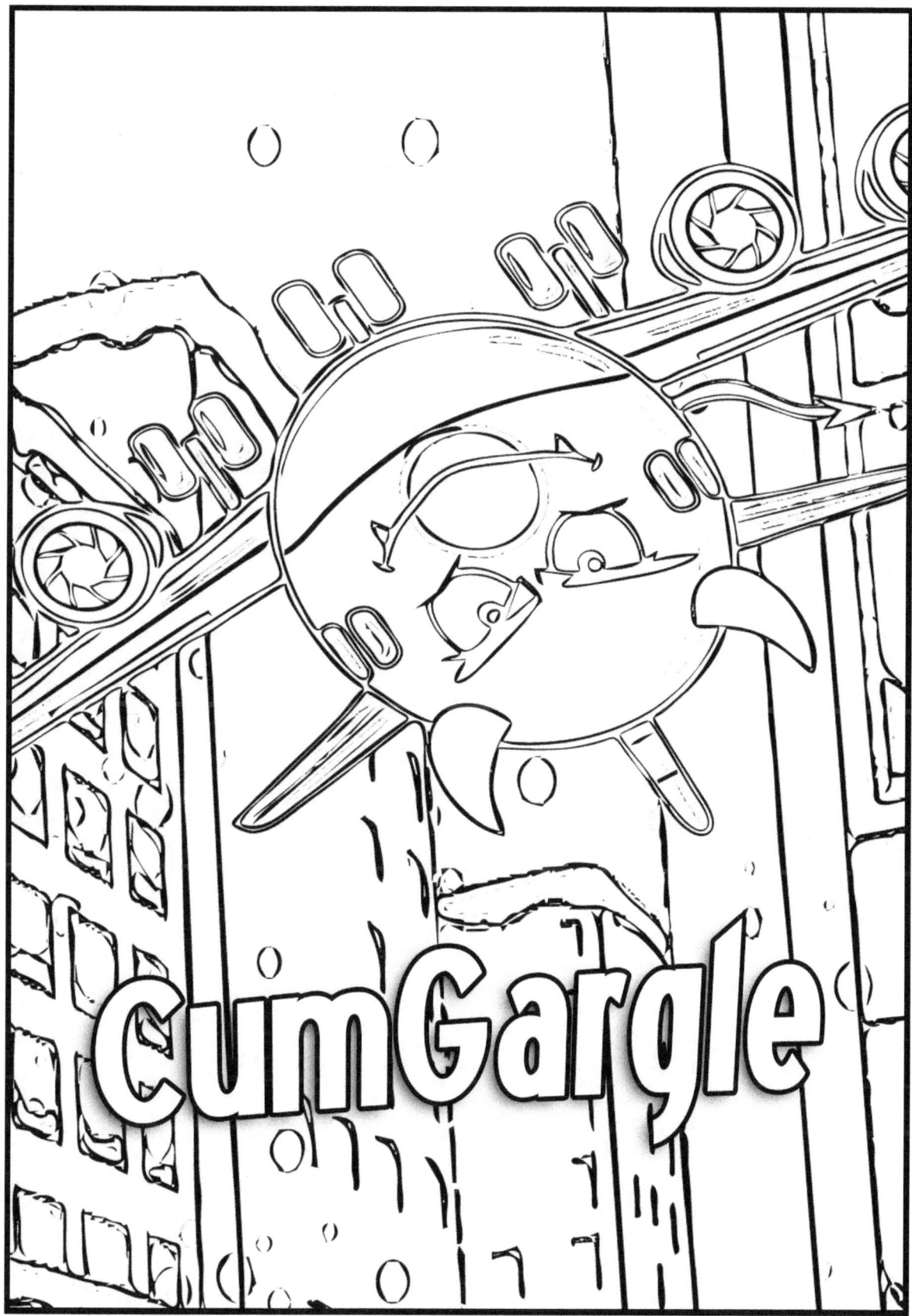

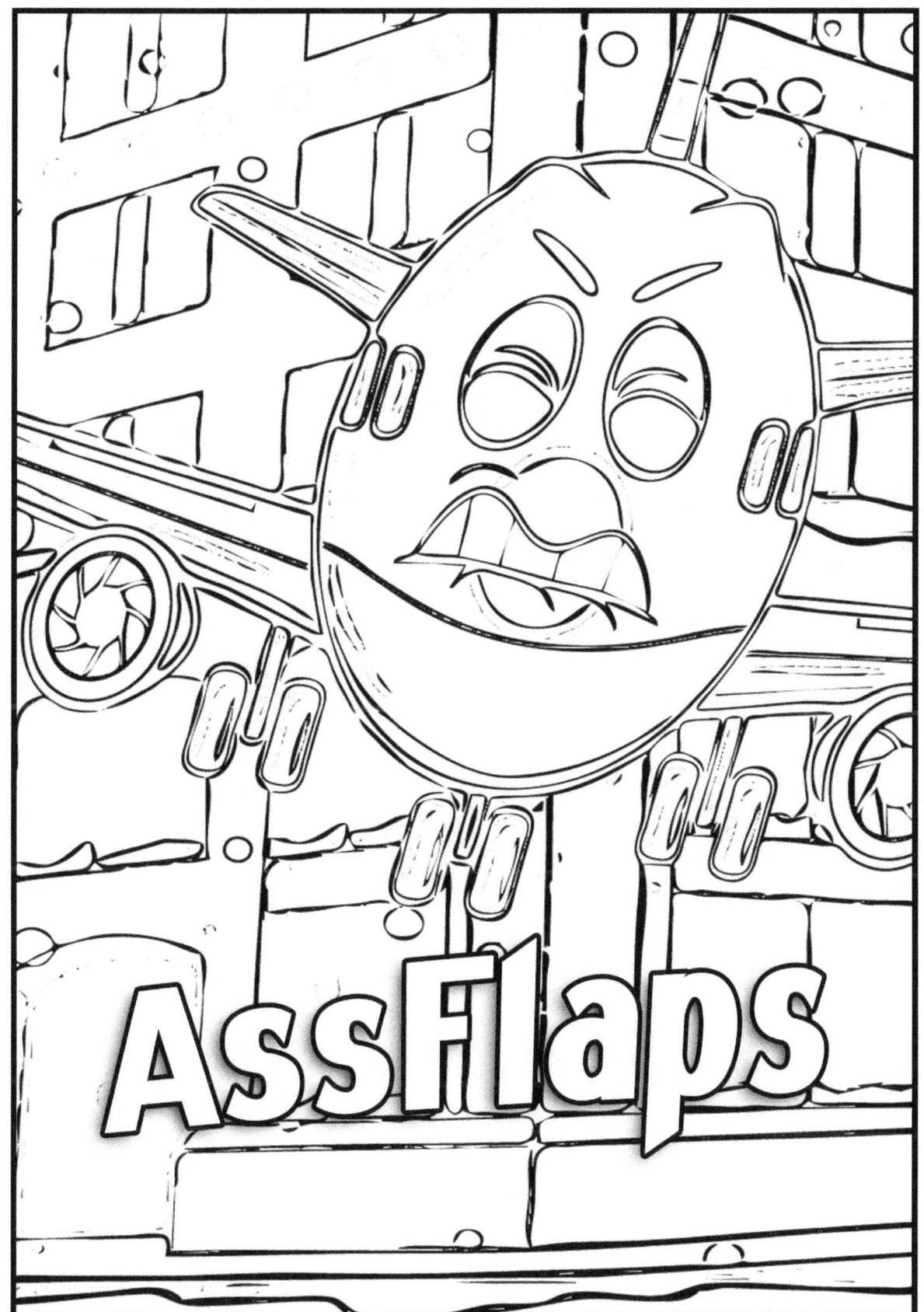

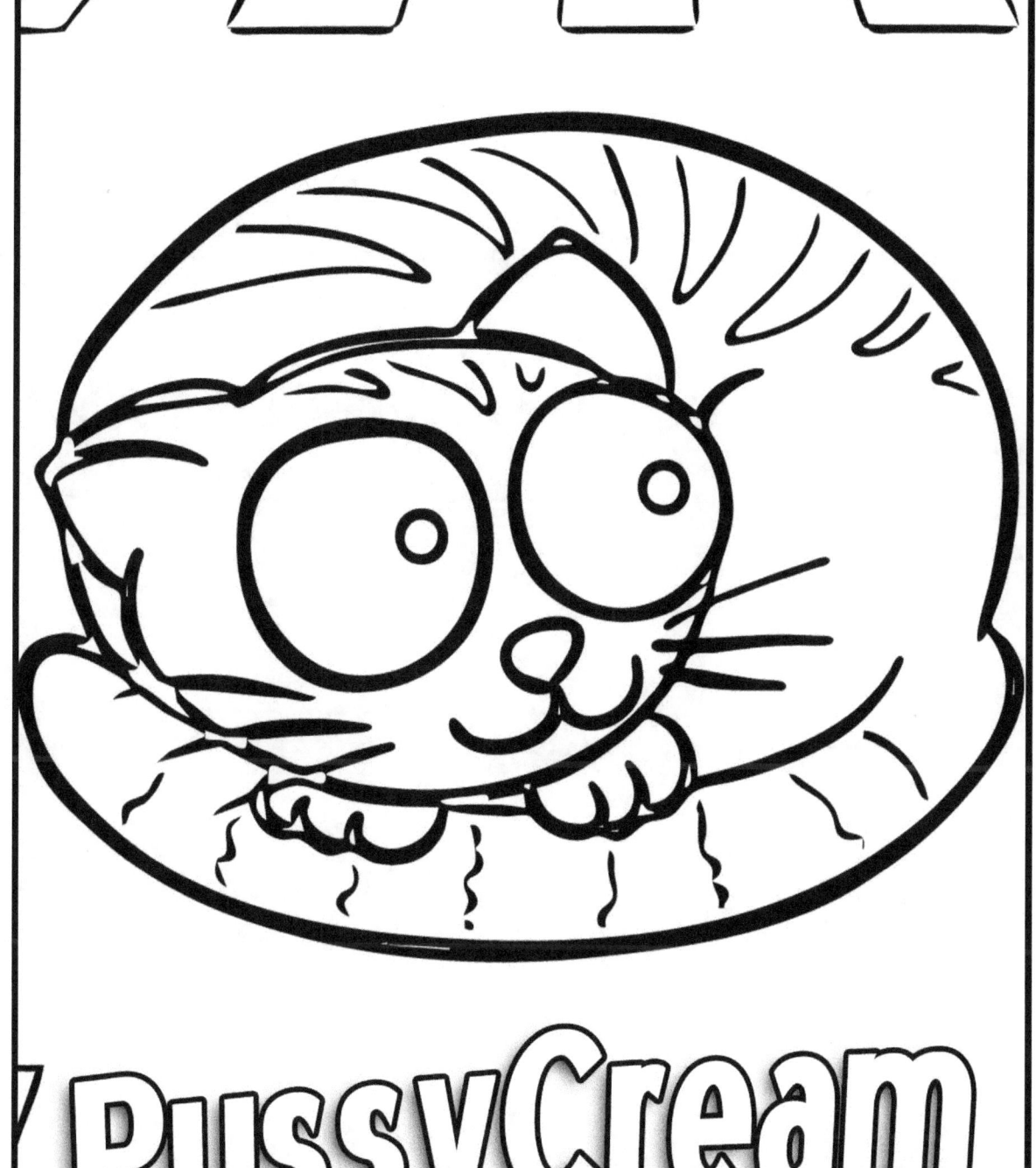

PussyCream

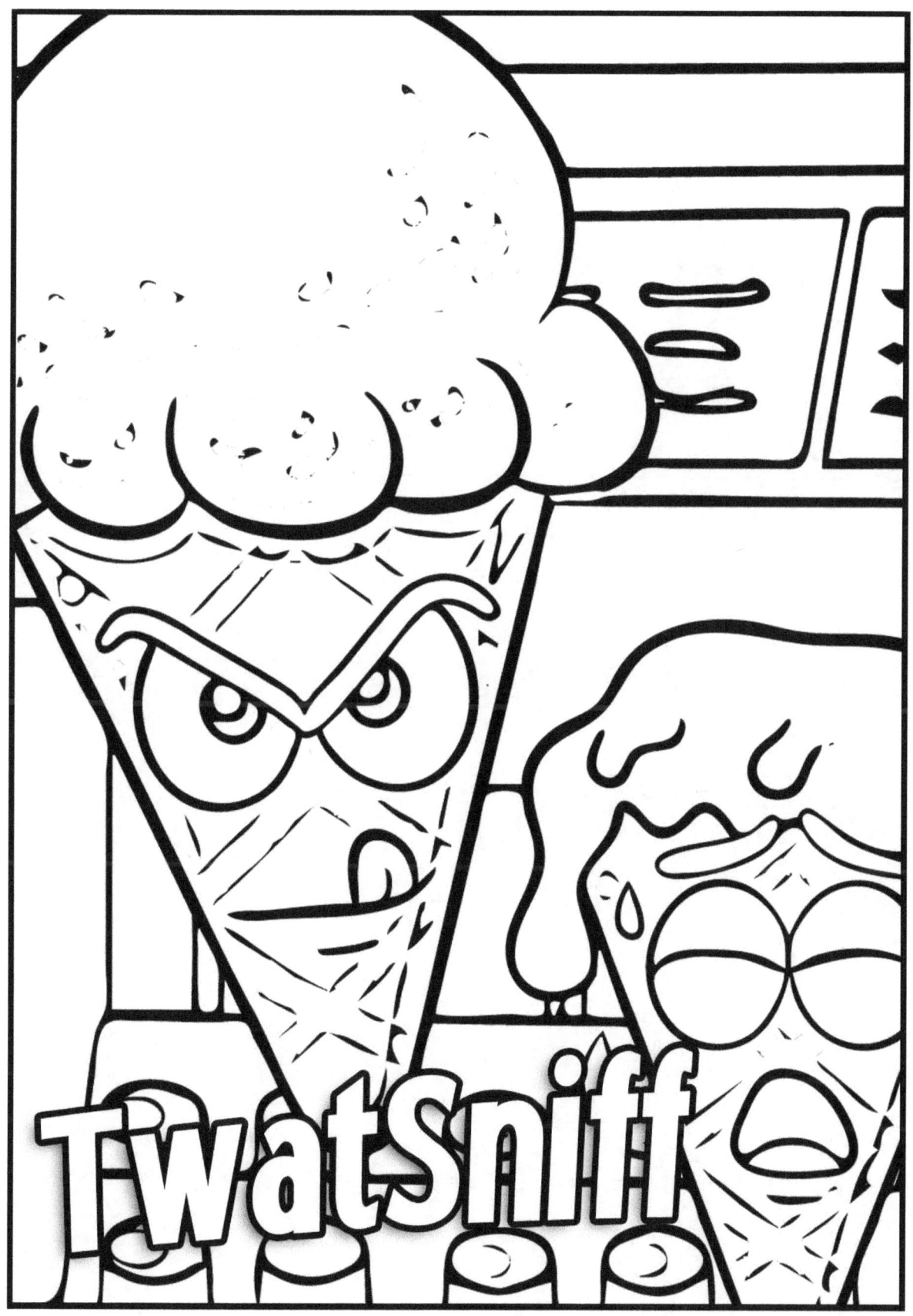

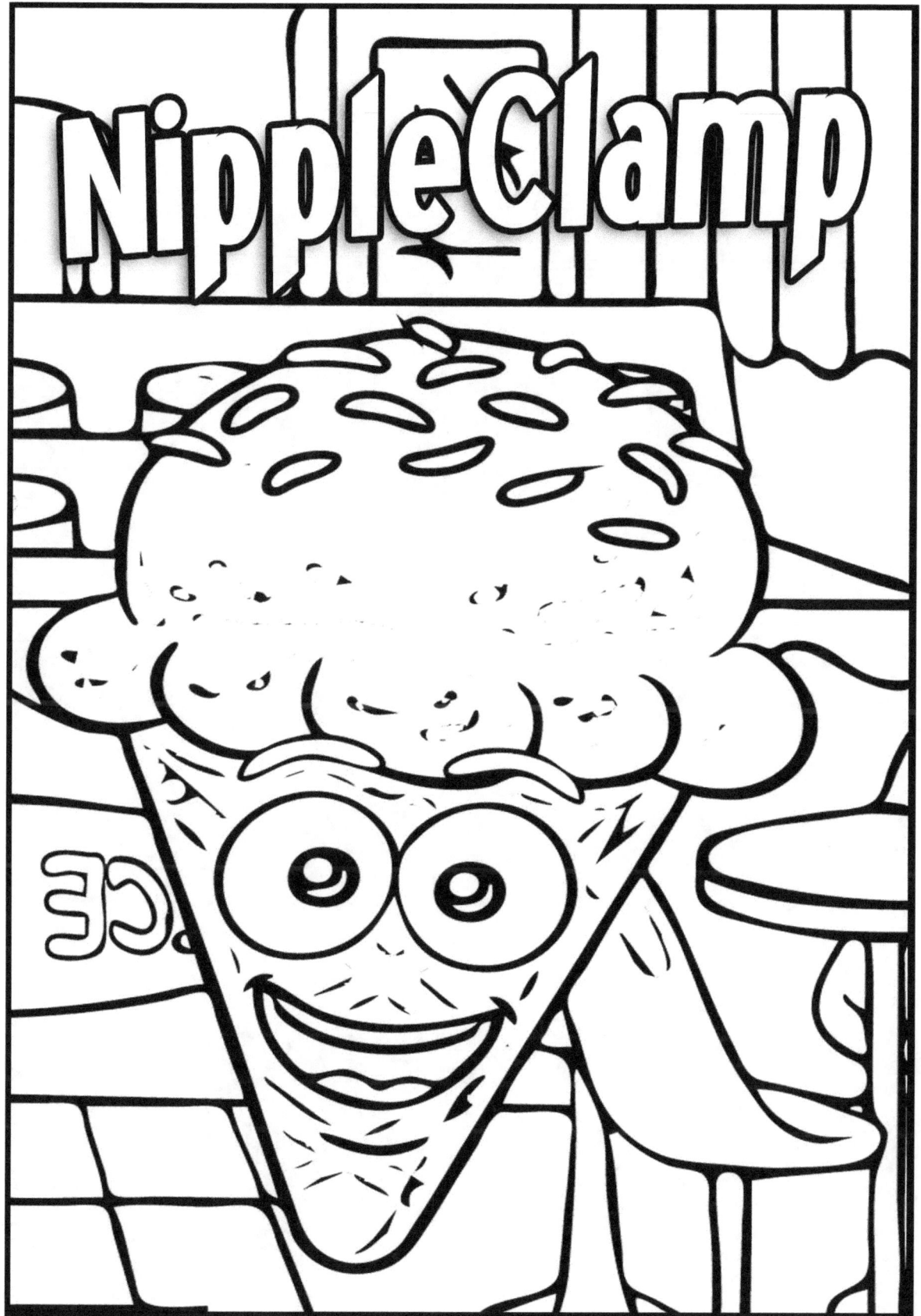

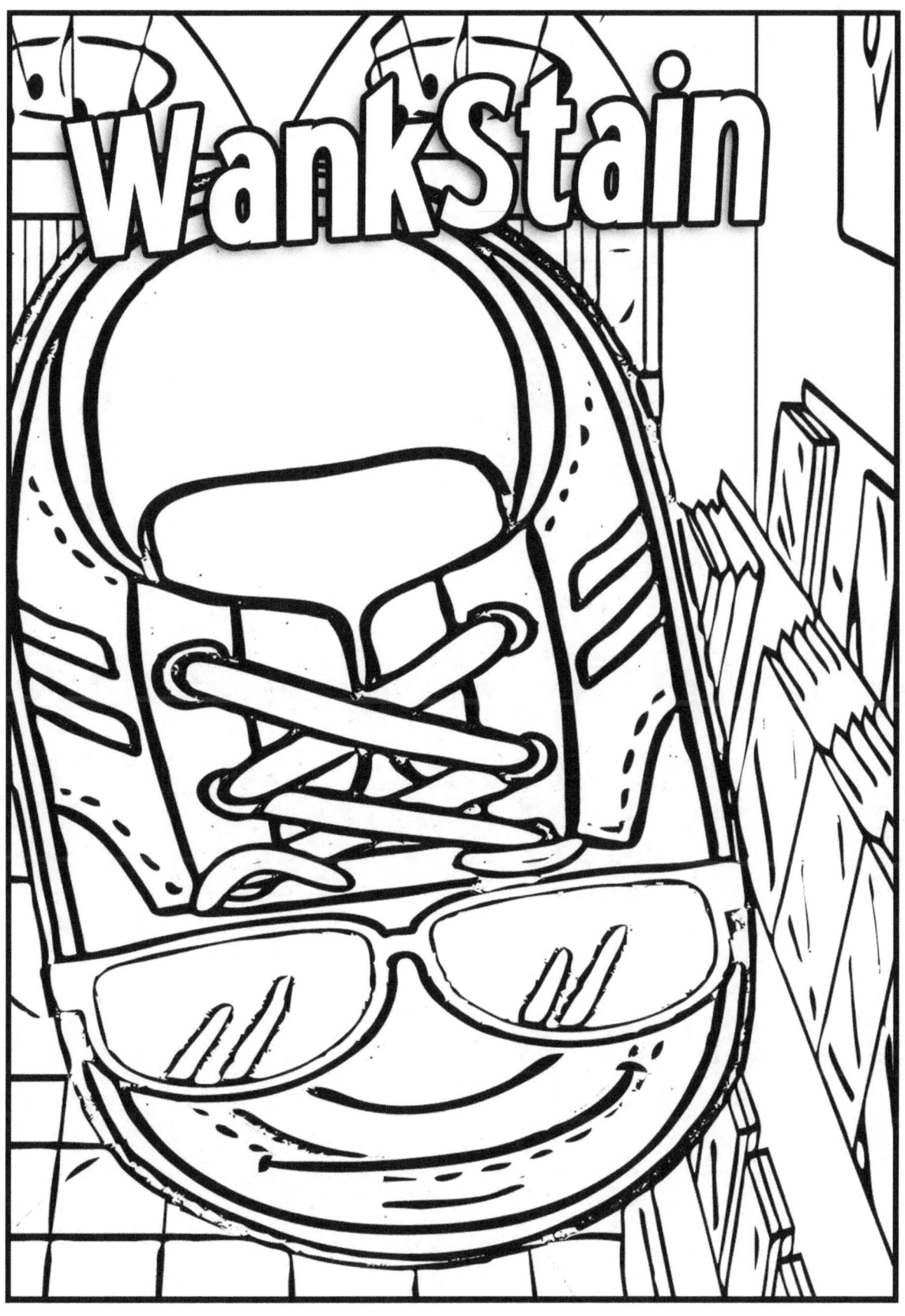

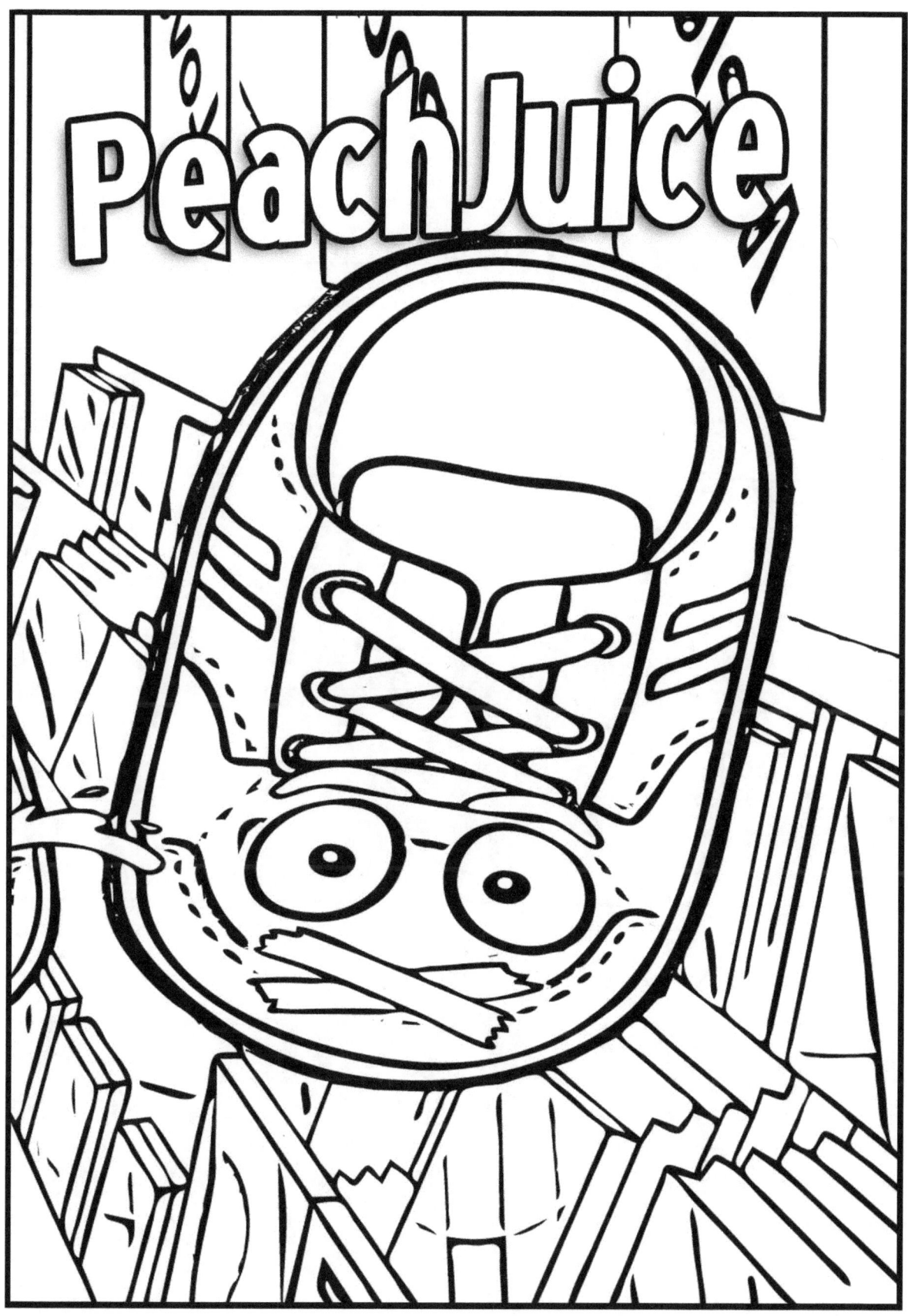

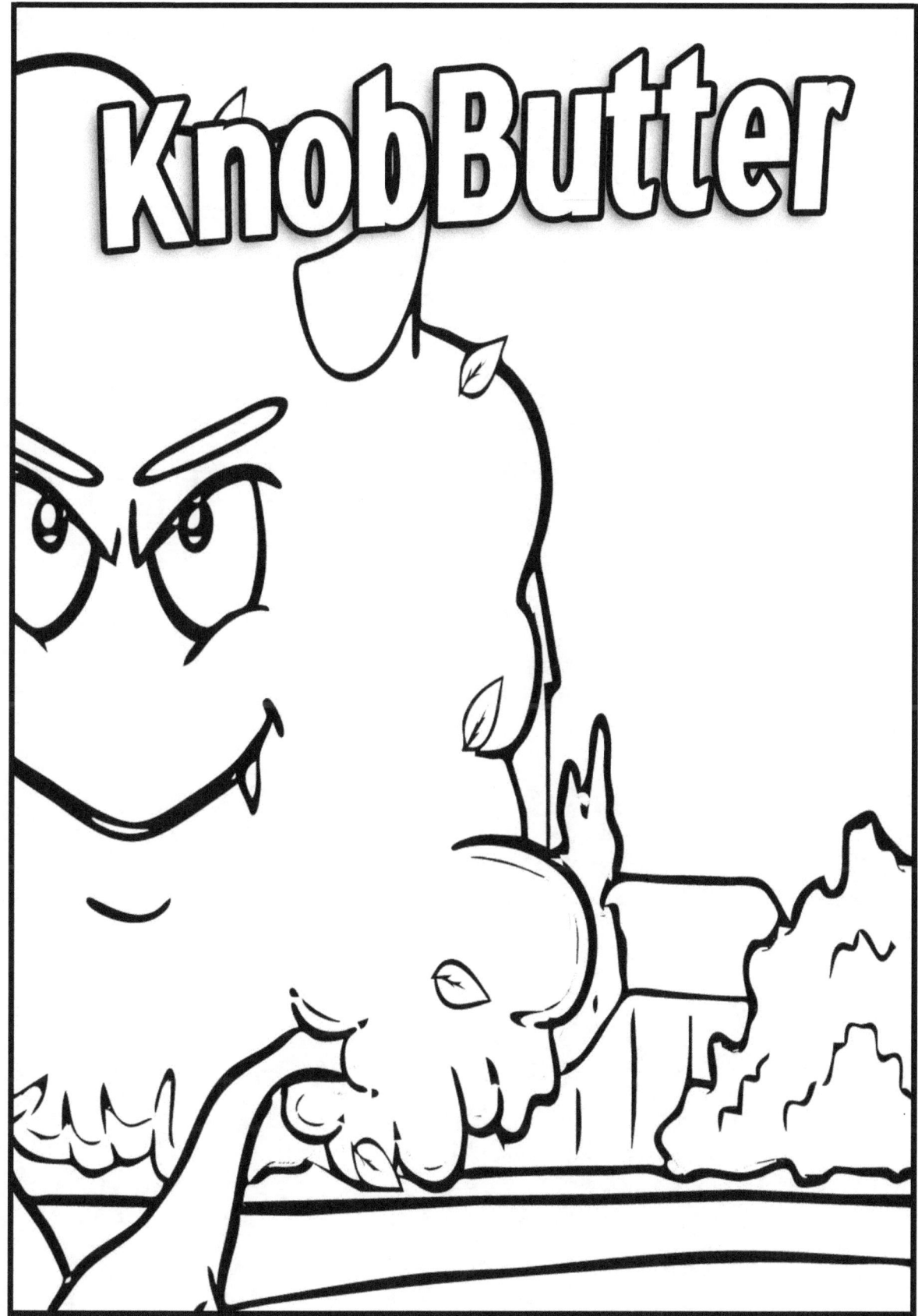

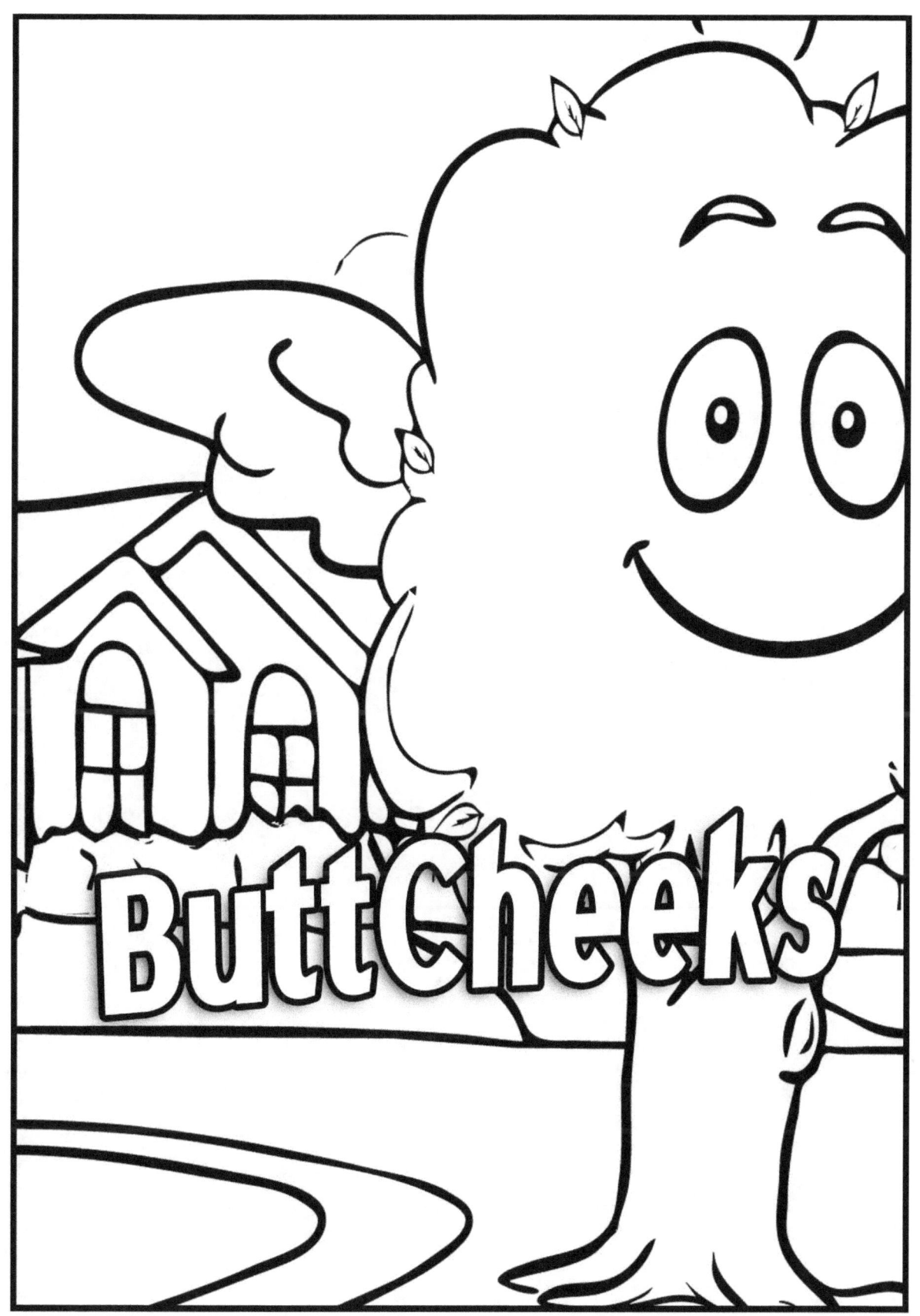

SquirtBucket

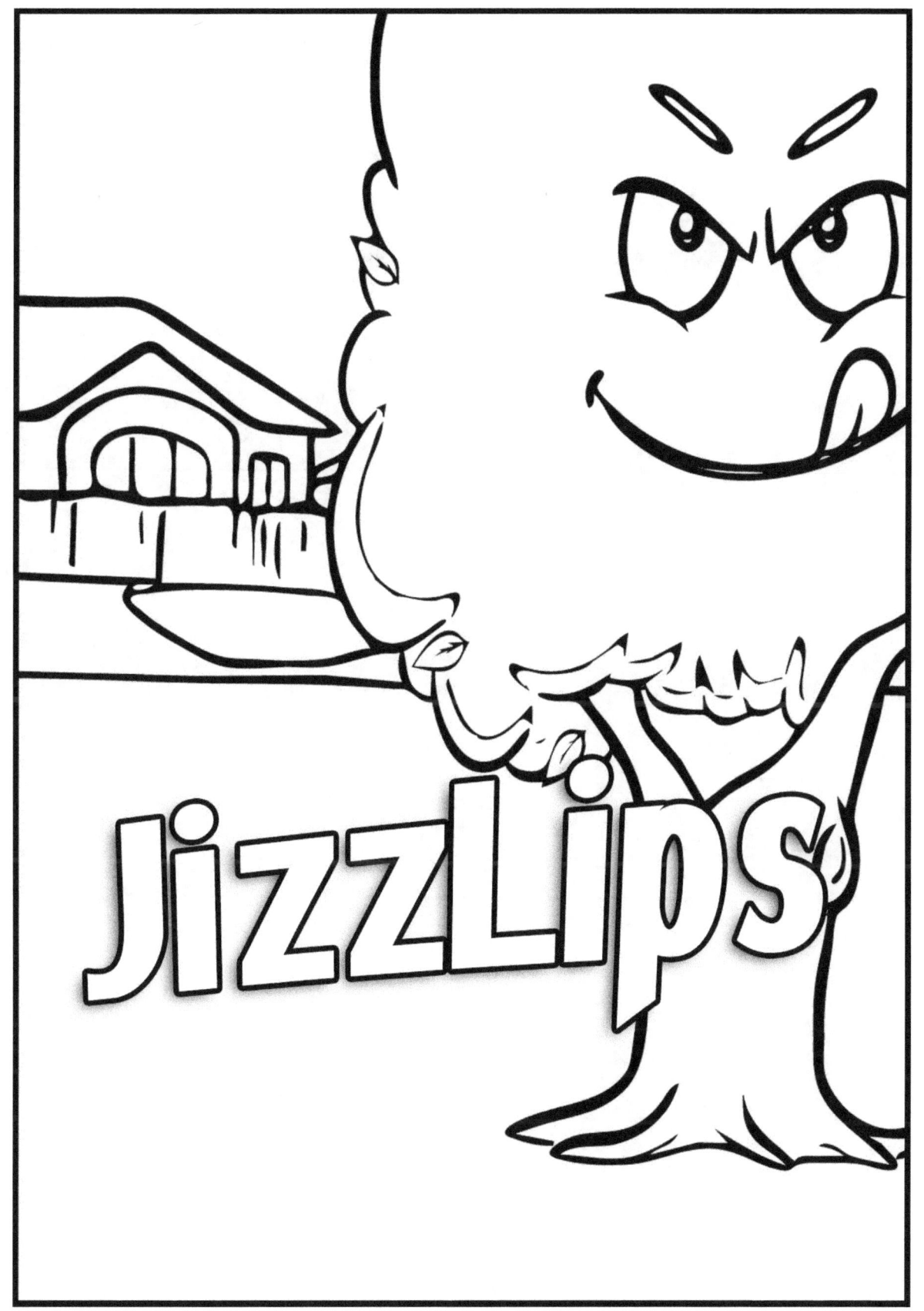

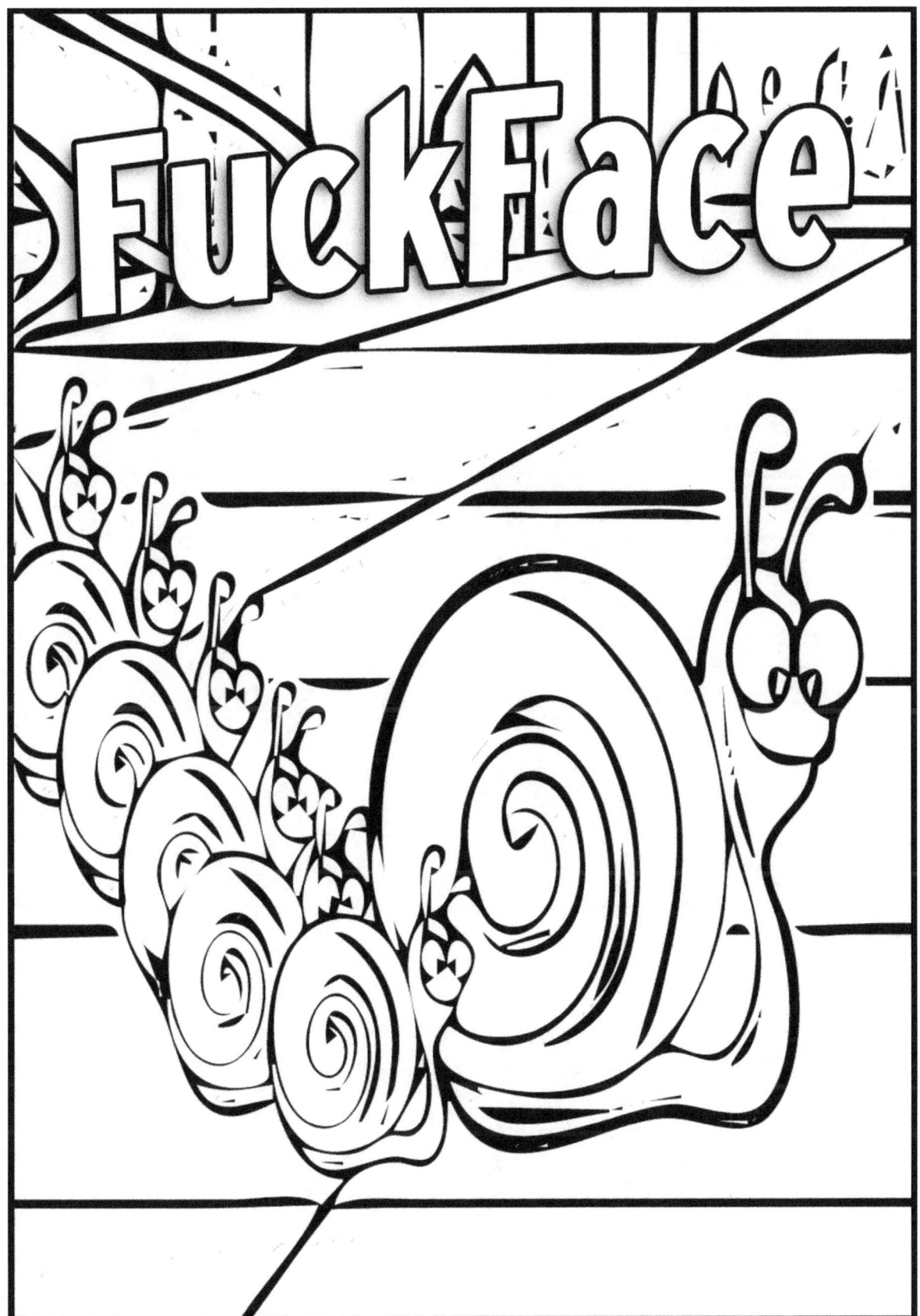

www.ingramcontent.com/pod-product-compliance
Lightning Source LLC
Chambersburg PA
CBHW080612190526
45169CB00007B/2975